Letters *from* Heaven

Comfort for Those Who Are Hurting

CLAIRE CLONINGER

HONOR **HB** BOOKS

Inspiration and Motivation for the Season of Life

COOK COMMUNICATIONS MINISTRIES
Colorado Springs, Colorado • Paris, Ontario
KINGSWAY COMMUNICATIONS LTD
Eastbourne, England

Honor Books® is an imprint of
Cook Communications Ministries, Colorado Springs, CO 80918
Cook Communications, Paris, Ontario
Kingsway Communications, Eastbourne, England

Letters from Heaven: Comfort for Thoses Who are Hurting
© 2003 by Claire Cloninger
Represented by: Alive Communications, Inc.
7680 Goddard Street
Suite 200
Colorado Springs, Colorado 80920

Printed in Canada
Printing / Year
8 7 6 5 4 / 05 06 07

ISBN: 1-56292-784-1

Dedication

One of my life's best blessings is a very gifted and loving group of siblings. This book is dedicated with love and gratitude to my sisters, Ann and Alix; as well as my brothers, Johnny and Charlie.

Introduction

In *The Book of Common Prayer,* there is an intercession for "all whose lives are closely linked with ours." Not long ago it occurred to me that this is an intercession that applies to everyone, for we are all closely linked to one another by the common bond of our humanity. All of us are born, and all of us die. We all experience joy and sadness, hope and despair. And eventually, all of us find ourselves deeply in need of God's comfort, His courage, and His overcoming love.

I don't know where you are today. Perhaps you are facing a personal tragedy—the death of someone you love, an illness, or a divorce—and you desperately need to hear God's voice. Perhaps you are watching someone you love struggle with overwhelming problems and you long to bring the hope of God's words into that loved one's heartache. Or perhaps there is someone you hardly know who carries a silent loneliness—the loneliness of one who does not yet know the intimate love of the Father.

Letters from Heaven was written to speak into all of those kinds of situations. Each letter is based on a passage of scripture. Each was written with the firm belief that God is longing to bring His answers to our questions and His healing to our hurts. And most of all, each letter reflects my belief that our Father longs for the day when we will realize and rejoice in the fact that our lives are "closely linked" with His.

Claire Cloninger

Unlock My Word

He holds everything together
with his powerful word.

HEBREWS 1:3

The words I told you are spirit,
and they give life.

JOHN 6:63

My Precious Child,

When you feel your heart coming apart at the seams, you will find the power to hold it together in My Word. My Word is far more than mere words on paper. It is a wonderful mystery—a written transcript of My faithfulness. It is spirit and life for those who will search out its message.

But know this as you read: the riches of My Word can only be unlocked by My Holy Spirit, who will act as an interpreter for you. My Spirit not only knows the intent of My words, but He also knows the needs in your heart. That is why He can guide you in understanding what is written. And He can point your hurting heart to the One who lives to save and befriend you—my Son, Jesus.

Oh, My child, come and mine the gold that is here for you. Come and discover the life. Come embrace the Spirit and find the truth.

My Word is for you,
God

There Is a Place for Your Pain

God loved the world so much that he gave
his one and only Son so that whoever believes
in him may not be lost, but have eternal life.

JOHN 3:16

You will know that God's power is
very great for us who believe. That power
is the same as the great strength God
used to raise Christ from the dead.

EPHESIANS 1:19-20

My Own Child,

Do you know yet that there is a place for your pain? There is a cross where My Son, Jesus, was nailed for every sad, sinful thing in this world. He took it all into His body. Like a sponge, He drank up all the darkness and death in this universe and then died with it. And on a Sunday morning when His friends were still crying for the loss of Him, He arose! He came back and cut a bright, golden path through the thorns of remorse and hopelessness. Can you believe that? Can you grasp the reality that He is who I say He is? Can you accept what He did for the love of you?

Step out into that place called faith. Lift the heaviness of your sin, the stabbing pain of your sorrow, up to Him. See Him absorb it all into His brokenness. Sit still with open hands and say "yes" to Him: "Yes, I want this new life You are holding out to me. Yes, I want to belong to You, to wear the name of 'Christian,' to walk with You through this desert of despair and out into the springtime of Your resurrection." Can you say these words? If so, there is a new life waiting for you, My child.

Your Father and His,
God

I Will Come to You

God lives forever and is holy.
　　He is high and lifted up.
He says, "I live in a high and holy place,
　　but I also live with people who are
　　sad and humble.
I give new life to those who are humble
　　and to those whose hearts are broken."

ISAIAH 57:15

Acceptance

My Own Dear Child,

I wonder if you have any idea how near I am to you. Perhaps you picture Me high up in the clouds of Heaven, seated on a golden throne, surrounded by a deafening chorus of alleluias. How will He ever hear my small, sad voice? *you may wonder.* What does He know or care about one person's solitary pain?

Oh, My child, please believe Me; I hear every whispered word you pray. I see every single tear you shed. For though My home is in the highest heaven, I can also live here with you, as close as your closest friend. And if you unlock the door to your heart's hidden room, I will come in and dwell there and bring the peace and power of My Spirit with Me. And I will spread abroad My love that has known you from before the earth's foundations. I will dry your tears and share your heartaches, and I will bring with Me a gift that in time you will unwrap and put on. It is a garment of praise.

So turn to Me. Share your pain with Me. Invite Me into your broken heart.

I will come to you,
God

Nourish My Love in You

The desert and dry land will become happy; the
desert will be glad and will produce flowers.
Like a flower, it will have many blooms. It will
show its happiness, as if it were shouting with
joy. It will be beautiful like the forest of
Lebanon, as beautiful as the hill of Carmel and
the Plain of Sharon. Everyone will see the glory
of the Lord and the splendor of our God.

ISAIAH 35:1-2

My Child,

In a jungle thick with vines and tangled undergrowth, a single flower could be easily overlooked. But in the starkness of a desert, that flower becomes a focal point of great beauty.

It is much the same with My love in your life. When your days are filled with a mad tangle of relationships and activities, it is easy for you to overlook My love. But here in the desert of your days, you cannot overlook it. Your eyes are drawn to the bright blossom of My mercy growing up through your heart's desolation.

If you will use this season of sadness to tend My love, to water it with your tears, to nourish it with prayer and quiet times in My Word, its roots will go deep, and it will grow strong. Then a garden of hope will begin springing up where a desert of despair used to be, and many will be drawn to Me by the life they see in you.

Nourish my love,
God

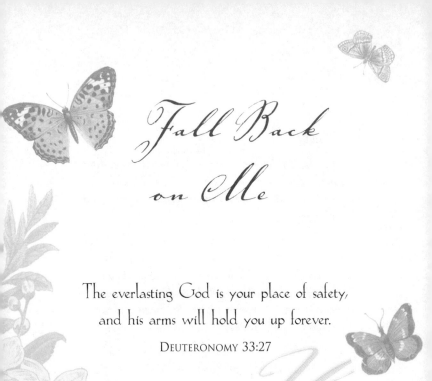

Fall Back on Me

The everlasting God is your place of safety,
and his arms will hold you up forever.

DEUTERONOMY 33:27

Dearest Child,

When your heart is overwhelmed and you need a place to hide, run to Me. I am your refuge, your place of safety where healing and mercy abound. When you feel that you cannot stand on your own for a moment longer, fall back on Me. Just beneath your deepest despair, My arms are waiting to catch you. My love is waiting to provide shelter. In this quiet place, you are free to be yourself—to cry or to sleep, to remember or to forget, or simply to get away for a time.

You are free to get away from the complications of your life, away from the eyes and the questions of those who do not understand the tender wounds you hold within. What a comfort to come to a place where you don't have to explain! Where you are fully known and fully accepted as you are. Here in this place of refuge, you can kick off your shoes and be your real self. You can say whatever is on your heart. I'm here to listen. You can ask whatever is on your mind. My love is strong enough to handle your questions and your doubts.

You can show Me your wounds. My mercy is strong enough to heal you. Run to Me. Fall back on Me. My arms are waiting.

Your Rest and Your Refuge,
God

Navigate by the Morning Star

I am the Root and the Offspring of
David, and the bright Morning Star.

REVELATION 22:16 NIV

Later, Jesus talked to the people again, saying,
"I am the light of the world. The person
who follows me will never live in darkness
but will have the light that gives life."

JOHN 8:12

My Own Dear Child,

Grief has many faces. In the swirl of strong emotions that follows a loss, some days you may feel angry and other days, sad. Some days you may feel hopeless and other days, surprisingly hopeful. And because these emotions are so strong, you may be tempted to navigate your journey of grief by their readings.

But that would be like a sailor trying to navigate his boat by a lightning bolt or a ray of sunshine rather than a compass. Though your emotions may rage like a hurricane, your heart can stay on course. For you have a compass on this journey. It is the light and the love of My Son, Jesus. Just as sailors of old could guide their boats by the North Star, your life will be aimed in the right direction if you let Jesus be your guiding light.

He who called himself "the bright Morning Star" will hold you steady through the storm of emotions. He will lead you into the safe harbor of My arms.

Navigate by the
Morning Star,
God

Face into Your Grief

There is a time for everything,
    and everything on earth has
    its special season.
There is a time to be born
    and a time to die.
There is a time to plant
    and a time to pull up plants.
There is a time to kill
    and a time to heal.
There is a time to destroy
    and a time to build.
There is a time to cry
    and a time to laugh.

ECCLESIASTES 3:1-4

My Dear Child,

I know your heart is heavy today. You look at the sun and wonder how it can shine in the face of your despair. How can the days and nights continue their steady progression of coming and going? *you wonder.* How can children laugh and flowers bloom when your heart is breaking?

I would say to you that this is their season for laughing and for blooming. But this, My child, is your season for grieving. Do not despise this season. Do not try to hurry it or hide it under the distraction of other things. Do not turn away from your sorrow or dry your tears too quickly. Do not fear your grief, but face into it. Feel it; learn its lessons; and let it run its full course in you. And look to Me through it all, My child, to comfort and uplift you; I will be here.

Your Friend and Father,
God

Let My Spirit Take Over

My grace is sufficient for you, for my
power is made perfect in weakness.

2 CORINTHIANS 12:9 NIV

When the Holy Spirit comes to you,
you will receive power.

ACTS 1:8

Dear Child,

When you're feeling in control of your life, it is difficult to surrender; but when things are out of control, surrender becomes easier. When you're on the winning side, there's no need to let go; but when you have suffered a loss, surrender is what you were designed for. Letting go is a lesson you were born to learn.

So let go, and give My Holy Spirit permission to take hold. He can work in you with a grace that may surprise you. He can get you through these difficult days by being a comforter, a companion, and a guide—always pointing you in the direction of My Son. And if you give Him the reins of your life in this sad season and watch Him work, I don't believe you will ever want to take them back into your own frail hands.

Come to Me in prayer. Make My Spirit welcome in you, and you will find that My grace working through Him, in you, is able to do much more than you could ever do on your own.

Let Him take over,
God

Let Us Travel Together

It was by faith Abraham obeyed God's call
to go to another place God promised to give
him. He left his own country, not knowing
where he was to go . . . like a foreigner. . . .
Abraham was waiting for the city that has real
foundations—the city planned and built by God.

HEBREWS 11:8-10

Now we see a dim reflection, as if we were
looking into a mirror, but then we shall see
clearly. Now I know only a part, but then I
will know fully, as God has known me.

1 CORINTHIANS 13:12

My Child,

Moving through this time of pain, you are like a stranger traveling through a foreign country. Though the landscape around you has not literally changed, suddenly everything seems different. One day your world is familiar and safe; and the next it is strangely altered by the reality of your circumstances, draped in the blue-gray shadows of sorrow. All that once felt solid, strong, and unshakably certain is suddenly swaying and lurching toward the unknown.

How can you make it through this bleak, uncertain season? Like Abraham, who was called out across a desert to a place he had never seen, you, too, are called to traverse this desert time. And, like Abraham's, yours is to be a journey of faith. But you will not travel alone. As I was with Abraham, so will I be with you.

Though you will never forget this time of pain, you will one day see it from the other side. For your destination is a city with real foundations, a city I myself have planned and built. There all shadows will be dispelled, all questions answered, and you will know me fully, even as you have been fully known by Me. Come . . .

> Let us travel together,
> God

Your Silence Will Be a Prayer

Why am I so sad?
Why am I so upset?
I should put my hope in God
and keep praising him. . . .
The Lord shows his true love every day.
At night I have a song,
and I pray to my living God.

PSALM 42:5, 8

Be quiet and know
that I am God.

PSALM 46:10

Dear Child,

I look upon your heart and see your sadness. I search your soul and know its despair. You turn to Me but cannot find the words to pray. You look to Me but cannot find the song to sing. Do not worry, child of Mine. I know all that is within you, and I understand. For now, your silence will be a prayer to Me and your tears, an offering.

I do not wish for you to act a part. I do not require a spiritual charade. But bring Me, instead, your real feelings, your brokenness, yourself. That is what I wait for, and I will meet you in the silence. There I will stay with you and heal your heart. And later, when the music has returned to your life, you will look back in love and recall this silent song we sang together.

Be quiet and know Me,
God

rgiveness

I Stand Between You and the Wind

A bruised reed he will not
break, and a smoldering
wick he will not snuff out.

ISAIAH 42:3 NIV

Acceptance

Dear Child of Mine,

As you go through this day, know that I am gently protecting you. I am as near to you as your very breath, as close to you as your heartbeat. I can see the fragile state of your emotions. I know how close to the surface your tender feelings are. I am aware that the wick of your spirit's inner light is flickering in the winds of your dilemma.

But you are My child, and I am on your side today. I will not allow the flame of your spirit to be snuffed out. I will stand between you and the wind. I will hold you in My love until you are strong again. Do not be troubled or afraid. Do not strive in your own strength, but lean into My love. Be strengthened by My Spirit. Find comfort in My mercy.

Your Shield and Defender,
God

Send out
the Dove

The dove could not find a place
to land because water still covered the
earth, so it came back to the boat. . . .
After seven days Noah again sent out the
dove from the boat, and that evening it came
back to him with a fresh olive leaf in its mouth.

GENESIS 8:9-11

My Dear Child,

Are you feeling caught in the currents of grief, cut off from life as you once knew it? Perhaps you have just begun to realize that because of your loss, your life will never again be exactly what it was before.

This is a fact you must accept and a reality you must grieve. Enter the ark of My protection as you grieve, and go with the currents of your sorrow for a season. But I encourage you, My child, to believe that after this flood of sorrow, there will be good times again. Not right away, perhaps, but in time.

Just as Noah sent out the dove to bring back a sign of dry land, I encourage you, in time, to send out the dove of My Holy Spirit to bring you a sign. He may return to you many times (as the dove did to Noah) with nothing. But when the season for hope and healing has come, He will return to you with a sign that it is time to come out of your ark and enter the land of the living once more.

And remember this: Wherever you are today, I am with you—whether in the ark or on dry land.

Through It All,
God

My Door Is Always Open

Lord, I call to you. Come quickly.
Listen to me when I call to you.
God, I look to you for help.
I trust in you, Lord. Don't let me die.

PSALM 141:1, 8

Let us, then, feel very sure that we can come
before God's throne where there is grace.
There we can receive mercy and
grace to help us when we need it.

HEBREWS 4:16

Dearest Child,

You must learn the liberty of being My child. David was not shy about telling Me his needs. He did not tiptoe into My presence, groveling for a crumb of mercy. Instead, he burst into My throne room and cried out for all the grace and power he needed.

You are no less a child of Mine than David was. In fact, in some ways you have easier access to Me than he did. For you can come to Me "in Christ." When My Son wishes to enter My presence, I delight to see Him, and I am quick to answer His requests. When you are in Him, you have that same easy access to Me—that of a child to a loving parent.

So do not hold back. Come boldly and tell Me your need. You will not be turned away.

My door is always open,
God

Pour Out Your Pain

Lord, hear my prayer;
listen to my cry for mercy.
Answer me
because you are loyal and good.

PSALM 143:1

A friend loves you all the time,
and a brother helps in time of trouble.

PROVERBS 17:17

Child of Mine,

Trying to hold your pain inside is like trying to build a dam across the ocean. The pressure of your emotions will build up within you until it cannot be contained, and it will break through in a torrent.

It is far better for you to vent your feelings as you feel them and to talk through your pain with someone you trust. You cannot pour out your pain to just anyone. You will not want to share your journey with everyone you know. Where, then, is the friend you can turn to and trust? You will recognize him by his loyalty. You will know her by her compassion. So be selective as you share your grief with those special few people in your life.

But there is one Friend you can come to anytime, day or night—one Friend who will never put you on hold or require you to make an appointment for some later date. I am that Friend to you, My child. I am here for you day or night, whenever you need to talk things through. So come to Me. Pour out your pain.

Your Friend Forever,
God

We Are Truly One

On that day you will realize that
I am in my Father,
and you are in me, and I am in you.

JOHN 14:20 NIV

You are all around me—in front and in back—and have put your hand on me. Where can I go to get away from your Spirit? Where can I run from you? If I rise with the sun in the east and settle in the west beyond the sea, even there you would guide me. With your right hand you would hold me.

PSALM 139:5, 7, 9-10

My Child,

Take comfort in this fact: You are in Me, and I am in you. This is a profound mystery and a secret that is known only by those who invite Me into their hearts.

How can you be in Me and I in you? Just as the air you breathe is all around you and also within you, so am I. You are in Me—in My spiritual atmosphere of grace and mercy that makes your spirit strong. And I am in you, the spiritual breath in your lungs by which you are sustained. During this difficult season, it is more important than ever for you to dwell in an awareness of this reality, for it will strengthen you when you are weak.

Don't you see? We are part of each other, and nothing can separate us; for I created you in My image to be in Me, and you have invited Me into your heart to be in you.

We are truly one,
God

You, Too, Will Overcome

"I have told you these things, so that in me you
may have peace. In this world you will have trouble.
But take heart! I have overcome the world."

JOHN 16:33 NIV

Those people will never be hungry again, and they
will never be thirsty again. The sun will not hurt
them, and no heat will burn them, because the Lamb
at the center of the throne will be their shepherd. He
will lead them to springs of water that give life. And
God will wipe away every tear from their eyes.

REVELATION 7:16-17

My Dear Child,

I know you were not prepared for this grief you are going through. But no one is ever prepared; for grief is an unknown darkness until you are in the midst of it.

Jesus spoke clear words of warning about the trouble that comes to every person on the human journey. He was well aware that trials are inevitable in this fallen and imperfect world. But He also gave precious words of encouragement to His beloved flock. "Take heart," He said, "for I have overcome the world!" What does this mean to you? It means that when you are in Him, you, too, will overcome. For in Him, you are moving toward a place where there will be no more hunger or thirst, no more grieving or trouble or pain. There, all will be healed and restored and set right. And there I will meet you and dry every tear from your eyes.

Take heart,
God

In Your Grief, I Grieve

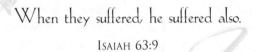

When they suffered, he suffered also.

ISAIAH 63:9

I will never leave you nor forsake you.

JOSHUA 1:5 NIV

Dear Child,

Do you think I can stand apart dispassionately watching you suffer without also feeling your pain? No. In your suffering, I also suffer. And in your grief, I am sorely grieved.

I am present with you during this trial. I stand beneath you as the solid ground when all else around you has become like shifting sand. I stretch out My love above you as a canopy, sheltering you from the rain. I stand behind you to catch you when you falter and fall; and I go before you to pave a path of light through the thick, dark clouds of despair. But most of all, I stand beside you as a Friend and a Father.

And so I would ask you today to do this one thing for Me, My child. See Me here—beneath you and above you, before you and behind you, and always at your side. See with eyes of faith, and know that I will never leave you nor forget you.

Forever,
God

Jesus Prays for You

I have prayed for you . . .
that your faith may not fail.

LUKE 22:32 NIV

Christ Jesus died, but he was also raised
from the dead, and now he is on
God's right side, begging God for us.

ROMANS 8:34

My Dear Child,

Would it surprise you to know that there are people praying for you today—people who care about the pain you feel and the struggle you are facing? Would it surprise you to know that My very own Son, Jesus Christ, is standing right beside Me today, speaking your name and asking Me to help you?

He is praying for you, as He prayed for His friend Peter, that you will not lose your faith during this trial. He is asking Me to grant you a special portion of mercy so you can come through this ordeal intact.

Believe Me when I tell you I listen to the voice of My Son and to the prayers of My people. They are for you, and I am for you. So be encouraged this day, My child.

You are surrounded by love,
God

I Am at Work in Your Trouble

We know that in everything God works for the good of those who love him. They are the people he called, because that was his plan.

ROMANS 8:28

Acceptance

Dear Child,

Do you know that I loved you before you even knew about Me? I carefully designed you and created you, and when I brought you into being, I called you to be My own. When you answered My call and returned My love and invited Me into your heart, what a joyful day that was for Me! I began right then to work in every part of your life to bring good to you—not only in the good parts or the slightly disturbing parts of your life, but even in the very worst parts of your life.

Even in the midst of this situation you are dealing with today, I am at work drawing good from the bad. I know it may seem impossible to imagine any good at all ever coming out of this pain in your life, but I am committed to doing this, and I will. The good I bring about will not erase the bad you have suffered. But it will be something new, something fresh and unexpected I will bring out of this painful situation—because you are Mine, because I called and you answered. I am at work, even in this.

Believe me,
God

You Are Precious in My Sight

He heals the brokenhearted and bandages their wounds. He counts the stars and names each one.

PSALM 147:3-4

Two sparrows cost only a penny, but not even one of them can die without your Father's knowing it. God even knows how many hairs are on your head. So don't be afraid. You are worth much more than many sparrows.

MATTHEW 10:29-31

Dear Child of Mine,

You may be tempted at times to think that I am too busy running the world and looking after the universe to have time for you and your pain. That couldn't be farther from the truth!

Don't you know you are very precious to Me? I'm never too busy for you. I know every hair on your head, every cell in your body. I designed you and brought you forth. I have a purpose and a plan for your life. How could I not intimately care for you, especially now?

My thoughts turn to you a million times a day. The pain you are feeling I am also feeling, for you are a part of Me. Daily, I am pouring My healing into your life so that in time you will be whole again. Carefully, I am looking after your heart's hidden wounds, tenderly touching them with healing hands of love. Come to Me often. Share your life with Me. For you are My own child, very precious in My sight.

Faithfully,
God

You Will Find Me Faithful

All the ways of the Lord are loving and faithful.

PSALM 25:10 NIV

The Lord does great things; those who enjoy them seek them. What he does is glorious and splendid, and his goodness continues forever. His miracles are unforgettable. The Lord is kind and merciful. He gives food to those who fear him. He remembers his agreement forever. Everything he does is good and fair; all his orders can be trusted. They will continue forever. They were made true and right. He sets his people free. He made his agreement everlasting. He is holy and wonderful.

PSALM 111:2-5, 7-9

Dearest Child,

What I have spoken is so. All of My ways are loving and true. Can you believe that? Just now you may be thinking that all of them are loving and true . . . except the difficult and painful path you are on today. But I am assuring you that all of My paths are cleared by My love and paved with My faithfulness—every one of them.

I am asking you to take this word for yourself. Take it on faith. Own it. Write it out. Believe it. For though this path you are on seems strange to you, it is well known to Me. You see, My Son, Jesus, walked this path of pain before you, and on this path He found Me faithful. Rest in this reality. Lean on Me, and let My love fill you. Take courage, My child. You will find Me faithful too.

Forever your Father,
God

Release the Pain of Injustice

Here is my servant, the one I support. He is the one
I chose, and I am pleased with him. I have put my
Spirit upon him, and he will bring justice to all
nations. . . . He will truly bring justice; he will not
lose hope or give up until he brings justice to the
world. And people far away will trust his teachings.

ISAIAH 42:1, 3-4

God does not see the same way people see.
People look at the outside of a person,
but the Lord looks at the heart.

1 SAMUEL 16:7

My Beloved Child,

I know so well that life looks unfair to you at times. You struggle with the injustice in your life. Tears sting your eyes as you recall it, and bitterness wells up in your heart.

Hear Me, My child. No human being has the vision to see what is just or the power to bring pure justice. This is why I have asked you not to judge others. For you look on the outward appearance, but I, the Lord your God, look deeper. I look upon the heart.

And here is the good news: Into your midst One has been born who sees as I see—with pure justice rendered with rightness and tempered with mercy. He will not overlook the innocent or crush the weak. He will not be deceived by the cunning or intimidated by the ruthless. I have committed your case and every case under Heaven into His hands.

Release the pain of these injustices to Him, and forgive those who have wronged you. Then rest in the knowledge that justice will be done.

Trust Me on this, My child,
God

My Mercy Will Be Your Lifeboat

When you pass through the waters,
I will be with you.
When you cross rivers,
you will not drown.

ISAIAH 43:2

Acceptance

Precious Child,

There are times when your pain seems overwhelming—times when you feel as though you will drown in your sadness or be swept away by your sense of loss. Perhaps you have even felt frightened by the rivers of your own tears—afraid that if you let them begin to flow freely, they might never stop.

Do not fear these things, My child, for My love will hold you up in the deep waters of your sorrow. My mercy will be your lifeboat. Be confident of this today. I will not let you get in over your head. Turn to Me and share your heart with me. I am here for you.

Lovingly,
God

Grieve, but with Hope

Brothers and sisters, we want you to know
about those Christians who have died so you
will not be sad, as others who have no hope.

1 THESSALONIANS 4:13

Dear Child of Mine,

You are not to grieve like those who do not know Me as Father. You are not to grieve like those who do not know My Son as Savior. Your grief is to be different. It is to be infused with hope.

For you know that Jesus died and rose again, and this is to be the foundation of your hope as you grieve every loss in your life. He is the Lord over every loss and every heartache, and He is the Lord of all comfort and mercy. He is the Lord of resurrection, restoration, and regeneration. He is the Lord of Life!

And so, in your sorrow, I am asking you to do this one thing. Allow one bright pinpoint of light to enter your darkness. Allow one brilliant ray of hope to penetrate your gloom. Open the door of your wounded heart just an inch or two, and this hope that is yours in Christ Jesus will rush in, bringing with it His great, glad tidings.

"All is not lost!" He will say. "All is not finished; I have overcome the grave and risen to new life! I am the Lord of lost causes, the God of second chances, the One who died to bring you life!" Listen to your Savior's words.

He is your hope,
God

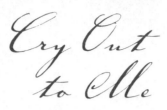

Cry Out to Me

Those people who know they have
great spiritual needs are happy, because
the kingdom of heaven belongs to them.

MATTHEW 5:3

I am very happy to brag about my weaknesses.
Then Christ's power can live in me. For this reason
I am happy when I have weaknesses, insults, hard
times, sufferings, and all kinds of troubles for Christ.
Because when I am weak, then I am truly strong.

2 CORINTHIANS 12:9-10

Get up, cry out in the night, even as the night begins.
Pour out your heart like water in prayer to the Lord.
Lift up your hands in prayer to him for
the life of your children who are fainting
with hunger on every street corner.

LAMENTATIONS 2:19

My Precious Child,

Today are you aware of your emptiness, your spiritual poverty, your personal neediness? Do you feel weak or in some way inadequate? Well, let Me tell you a wonderful secret of My kingdom. When you are most empty, the One who fulfills you is very near. When you are poor in spirit, great spiritual riches are at hand. When you are the most needy, the One who meets your need draws close to hear your cry.

For, you see, My kingdom is unlike any worldly kingdom. In this world's system, the soul who is poor, weak, needy, or empty is often despised and ignored. But in My kingdom, when you feel bound by great need, you are actually in a position to know the exciting truth that will free you. And here is that truth: Your need is the very thing that causes you to cry out to Me. And it is when you do cry out to Me that I will come into your heart and heal you and make you whole. So cry out to Me in your time of spiritual emptiness, and I will fill you with My own Spirit.

Your Heart's Supply,
  God

Receive the Peace of Christ

Peace I leave with you; my peace I give you.
I do not give to you as the world gives. Do not
let your hearts be troubled and do not be afraid.

JOHN 14:27 NIV

Do not worry about anything, but pray and ask God
for everything you need, always giving thanks. And
God's peace, which is so great we cannot understand it,
will keep your hearts and minds in Christ Jesus.

PHILIPPIANS 4:6-7

Christ came and preached peace to you
who were far away from God, and to
those who were near to God. Yes, it is
through Christ we all have the right to
come to the Father in one Spirit.

EPHESIANS 2:17-18

My Dear Child,

Today I remind you of an inheritance left to you by My Son on the last night of His earthly life. It is the gift of His peace. Did you know that as Jesus moved through the painful circumstances of His last hours on earth, His thoughts were of you? He desired more than anything that you should possess a peace beyond anything this temporary world can offer—a peace greater than the limits of your finite mind.

This peace can only be revealed by My Holy Spirit, who speaks to you in the language of the heart. Like a crystal-clear underground stream, this peace will flow through the deep places of your spirit, below the surface of your earthly pain, gently reminding you of a love that is eternal and a power that has overcome the grave. So do not let grief or pain or sorrow consume you. Do not allow fear to pull you under. Come to Me and possess your inheritance.

Receive the peace of Christ,
God

giveness

I Am the Song in Your Silence

The Lord your God is with you;
the mighty One will save you.
He will rejoice over you.
You will rest in his love;
he will sing and be joyful about you.

ZEPHANIAH 3:17

Acceptance

My Child,

Some days the pain you feel seems to cover you like a shroud. Some days it cuts like an icy wind. Some days the sound of your solitude blocks out the normal sounds of the day—the breeze in the trees, the birdsong, the rain.

My child, I am asking you to listen with your heart. Listen intently, and you will hear a song. It is the song of your Lord and your God. It is the song I am singing over you. You are My beloved one, and in you I find reason to rejoice.

Don't you see? Don't you understand yet? You are not alone, for I am with you. I am the mighty one whose hand is swift to save. I am the arms of love in which you will find welcome and rest. I am the quiet, inner music that sings in your spirit, the song of joy that is healing your broken heart. And even on those days when you feel alone and you cannot hear My music, please know, My child, that I am here.

The Song in Your Silence,
God

Bring Me
Your Emptiness

Jesus answered ". . . You give them something
to eat." They said to him, "But we have only five
loaves of bread and two fish." Jesus said, "Bring the
bread and the fish to me." . . . He took the five
loaves and the two fish and, looking to heaven, he
thanked God for the food. Jesus divided the bread
and gave it to his followers, who gave it to the
people. All the people ate and were satisfied. Then
the followers filled twelve baskets with the leftover
pieces of food. There were about five thousand men
there who ate, not counting women and children.

MATTHEW 14:16-21

My Dear Child,

Today I am asking you to bring Me all that you have. "But," you say, "I have nothing to bring, for I am spent and wrung out and desperately empty. I have nothing but heartache and inadequacy." Then that, My child, is exactly what I am asking you to bring.

You see, I want nothing from you but yourself, just as you are, feeling as you feel, hurting as you hurt. Just as Jesus asked His friends to bring their inadequate amount of food to Him, I am asking you to bring your inadequate amount of faith and hope and courage to Me. Just as his friends gathered up their scant supply of nourishment and took it to their Master, you must gather up your scant supply of inner strength and bring it to Me. For I will touch and break and transform your lack and hand it back to you as life and substance for the journey. So come now. Bring your emptiness to Me, and I will fill it with my Spirit.

I am here waiting,
God

Trust the Shepherd's Care

The Lord is my shepherd; I have everything I need.
He lets me rest in green pastures. He leads me to
calm water. He gives me new strength. He leads me
on paths that are right for the good of his name.
Even if I walk through a very dark valley,
I will not be afraid, because you are with me.
Your rod and your walking stick comfort me.
You prepare a meal for me in front of my enemies.
You pour oil on my head; you fill my cup to
overflowing. Surely your goodness and love will be
with me all my life, and I will live in the house of
the Lord forever.

PSALM 23:1-6

My Dear Child,

You are a lamb of My flock, a child in My care. Let Me lead you through this trying and painful time. Through quiet, green pastures I will lead you where you may rest and be refreshed. Along the banks of deep, cool waters I will guide you where you may drink deeply and be restored.

Do not fear this valley of sorrow, for I will surely uphold you through it all. I will prepare for you a table of blessing where the enemy of despair cannot touch you. Your cup will overflow with the joy of My abiding presence. And when the valley has been crossed, I will bring you out on the other side and lead you up again into the mountains of My mercy. Trust Me.

I am your Shepherd,
God

I Will Never Reject You

He was hated and rejected by people. He had much pain and suffering. People would not even look at him. He was hated, and we didn't even notice him.

ISAIAH 53:3

Since we have a great high priest, Jesus the Son of God, who has gone into heaven, let us hold on to the faith we have. For our high priest is able to understand our weaknesses. When he lived on earth, he was tempted in every way that we are, but he did not sin. Let us, then, feel very sure that we can come before God's throne where there is grace. There we can receive mercy and grace to help us when we need it.

HEBREWS 4:14-16

My Precious Child,

Nothing hurts worse than the pain of rejection. It hurts like a deathblow. Believe Me, I know. When Jesus walked the earth, He was hated and rejected by His own people. They were the very people He came to help, the very ones who should have loved Him most. But He was betrayed by Judas, one of his twelve best friends, and denied by Peter, perhaps His best friend of all.

And don't think that because He was My incarnate Son He didn't feel it. He felt the pain just as you do. His heart ached over those who turned from Him, and He had to deal with those feelings just as you do. So, today, if you are hurting as He hurt, draw near to Him, My child. Tell Him your feelings. Show Him your wounds. Ask Him to speak His healing words into your spirit, and then listen.

He will whisper comfort and courage and hope. He'll help you decide what needs to be decided, to speak what needs to be spoken, to forgive who needs to be forgiven, and to go on. Most of all, He will affirm what I am saying to you now: Though others may reject you, I never will. Never!

Faithfully,
God

It Is His Peace That You Require

Who is this? He commands
even the winds and the water,
and they obey him.

LUKE 8:25 NIV

Now may the Lord of peace give you
peace at all times and in every way.
The Lord be with all of you.

2 THESSALONIANS 3:16

Dearest Child,

Do you feel that the walls of your world have collapsed and you can no longer control the storms of circumstance outside nor the storms of emotion within? Do you feel outwitted and defeated and too overwhelmed to go on?

Don't despair. Don't give up. For truly, My Son, Jesus, can command even these things. He can bring order to your circumstances and a deep, sweet calm to your inner world. When He walked upon the earth, even the raging storms yielded to His voice. "Be still," were his words, and the wind obeyed.

He can still do these things, My child. He can speak these words into your life. It is His serenity you long for, His peace that you require. So come. Bring the storms of your life to Jesus, and let Him take control.

Trust Him!
God

Let Me Be Your Guide

Trust the Lord with all your heart,
and don't depend on your own understanding.

PROVERBS 3:5

If you go the wrong way—to the right
or to the left—you will hear a voice
behind you saying, "This is the right way.
You should go this way."

ISAIAH 30:21

Dear Child of Mine,

This is a time unlike any other you have gone through—a time in which you suddenly find yourself looking at life from a new perspective. It is as though everything has shifted and the boundaries of your world that were once so sure and secure seem somehow blurred and uncertain.

You may be tempted now to do something radical, to make some move or change in an effort to escape the pain you are in. But this is not a time for making big decisions. It is, instead, a time to stay still and wait until all of the dust has settled and you can accurately assess where you are. This is not a time to lean on your own understanding, but a time, more than ever, to trust in Me. I will help you know when to make any kind of move or change in your life. And in that day, it will be My voice behind you speaking softly to your spirit, saying, "This is the right way. Come, my child, and walk in it."

Let Me be your guide,
God

You Are a Part of Christ's Body

The human body has many parts. The foot might say, "Because I am not a hand, I am not part of the body." But saying this would not stop the foot from being a part of the body. The ear might say, "Because I am not an eye, I am not part of the body." But saying this would not stop the ear from being a part of the body. If the whole body were an eye, it would not be able to hear. If the whole body were an ear, it would not be able to smell. If each part of the body were the same part, there would be no body. . . . The eye cannot say to the hand, "I don't need you!" And the head cannot say to the foot, "I don't need you!"

1 CORINTHIANS 12:14-19, 21

Dear Child,

When your heart is breaking, it is easy to feel isolated. It is natural to see yourself as separate from those who are not going through the same kind of suffering. But I am asking you to remember that you are not alone. If you have put your faith in Jesus Christ, you are a part of Him. And that means you are also a part of the great host of believers who make up His body on earth. You may not feel that you are a part, but that does not change the fact that you are. And whether you realize it or not, you desperately need the other parts of the body, and they need you.

Think of your own body. Could you function at full capacity without a foot or a hand or an eye? Of course not! You need every member of your physical body terribly. In the same way, your brothers and sisters in Christ need you. They need to know what you are going through and how they can help. They need to understand your grief, for each of them will someday face it in his or her own life. Don't be afraid to share your pain. Don't be too proud to ask for help. Find your place in Christ's body.

You are surely a part,
God

He Will Carry Your Sorrows

He took our suffering on him and felt our pain for us. We saw his suffering and thought God was punishing him. But he was wounded for the wrong we did; he was crushed for the evil we did. The punishment, which made us well, was given to him, and we are healed because of his wounds.

ISAIAH 53:4-5

Dear Child,

*When your sorrow seems too heavy to hold, let it go.
Jesus will carry it for you. For surely He is the One who
takes up human suffering and carries human sorrows. Take
time today to be alone with Him. In a quiet place, lift your
heartache up in your hands as though it were wrapped in a
package. Lift it up to Him, and as your arms are lifted, tell
Him all that you are feeling. Describe to Him your pain.
Tell Him your anger. Give words to your feelings of despair.
Hold nothing back.*

*Leave your arms lifted up to Him until they ache as much
as your heart does, and when you feel you cannot hold that
package of grief up in your aching arms one moment longer,
see Jesus take it from you into His own strong, nail-pierced
hands. Then let your aching arms drop to your sides, and
feel the sweet release of that moment. And then, at the start
of each new day, remember that Jesus Christ is holding the
weight of your sorrow in His hands. Though you may
still have tears to cry, know that the weight of
your heartache belongs to Him now.*

Let Him hold your sorrows,
God

I Am Still Here

Don't worry, because I am with you.
Don't be afraid, because I am your God.
I will make you strong and help you;
I will support you with my right hand
that saves you.

ISAIAH 41:10

Acceptance

Dear Child,

Do you feel at times as though your life has somehow become enmeshed in thick clouds through which you can see no flicker of hope? I ask you to think, My child, of how often you have seen clouds cover the night sky, blotting out any sign of the stars. Did you think when this occurred that the stars had given up shining? Did you think they had burned out and tumbled into the blackness forever? No, that thought never crossed your mind, for you trust the constancy of the stars. You know that although they are hidden for a night they are still there, still shining, and you will see their light again.

Oh, My child, if you can trust the constancy of the stars, can you not trust the constancy of the One who created the stars and set them in space? Though My love may seem dim and distant to you now—blotted out by the clouds of your sorrow—I am still here, shining constantly down upon you, and I will always be. There is no darkness in this world so deep as to put out the light of My love.

Believe it!
God

Put the Past in My Hands

Song

If we confess our sins, he will forgive our sins, because
we can trust God to do what is right. He will
cleanse us from all the wrongs we have done.

1 JOHN 1:9

There is one thing I always do. Forgetting the past
and straining toward what is ahead, I keep trying
to reach the goal and get the prize for which God
called me through Christ to the life above.

PHILIPPIANS 3:13-14

Those who are in Christ Jesus
are not judged guilty.

ROMANS 8:1

Dear Child,

In the midst of your grief, do you find yourself sifting through the circumstances of your loss? Do the words "if only" often come to mind as you think again and again of things you wish you had done differently or ways you could have avoided this loss you are grieving?

Trust Me, My child. This kind of hindsight second-guessing can only tangle your mind and spirit in paralyzing cords of confusion and guilt. So I am asking you now to give up this futile self-condemnation. Instead, think clearly through these past events and be willing to acknowledge any sin on your part. Then come quickly to Me and confess that sin.

Whatever you confess, I will forgive. That is a promise. I have paid a precious price—the life of My only Son—for your freedom. Come now and let Me cut you free from this entangling snare of past regrets. Let Me forgive you and set your face toward the future.

Put the past in my hands,
God

You Need Not Stand Alone

Put on God's full armor. Then on the day
of evil you will be able to stand strong.
And when you have finished the whole
fight, you will still be standing.

EPHESIANS 6:13

The Lord stayed with me and
gave me strength.

2 TIMOTHY 4:17

Dearest Child,

There will be days when the fight is gone out of you, and you feel you cannot struggle anymore. There will be times when the weight of all you've had to bear has torn you up and worn you out, and the most you can do is to stand.

If that is where you are today, I ask you to know this: You need not stand alone. Today I will dress you in my armor so that you will be fortified against anything that comes against you. Perhaps it will only be a word, a memory, the wrong inflection of a voice, or some petty irritation that on any normal day would not faze you. But today, with your back against the wall, that small thing can come at you like an arrow. Don't let it hit your heart today. Let it hit the shield of faith I will give you to hold.

If you will do this, I promise you, you will not fall. And be certain of this, My child. I will be standing right here beside you, strengthening and defending you and helping you to stand.

Trust my strength,
      God

Hold My Promise in Your Heart

The sufferings we have now are nothing compared
to the great glory that will be shown to us.

ROMANS 8:18

All these great people died in faith. They did not get
the things that God promised his people, but they saw
them coming far in the future and were glad. They said
they were like visitors and strangers on earth. When
people say such things, they show they are looking for a
country that will be their own. If they had been
thinking about the country they had left, they
could have gone back. But they were waiting
for a better country—a heavenly country. So
God is not ashamed to be called their God,
because he has prepared a city for them.

HEBREWS 11:13-16

Dear Child,

I know the weight of the burden you are carrying. I understand your struggle and share your sorrow, for I am with you in the midst of it. That is why I long for you to understand something important.

This earthly life and its sorrows will not last forever. They will someday come to an end for you and for everyone, just as this earth itself will come to an end. But the life of the child who has trusted Jesus as Savior and known Me as Father has no end. Instead, My children will move from this earthly life of sorrow into a place of unending glory beyond anything the mind can imagine. Actually, there are no words in any earthly language that can explain or prepare you for the wonder of what awaits you there. The glory of that distant time even outweighs the grief of today. For there will be a sense of completeness on that day that will satisfy the aching emptiness of today.

So do not give up or give in. Have faith in the future I have prepared for you. Let Me comfort you and strengthen you and bring you healing. And all the while, hold in your heart this promise of the glory yet to come.

The One Who Loves You,
God

Listen to My Holy Spirit

"I will ask the Father, and he will give you another Counselor to be with you forever—the Spirit of truth."

JOHN 14:16-17 NIV

If Christ is in you, then the Spirit gives you life, because Christ made you right with God.

ROMANS 8:10

Acceptance

Dear Child,

Perhaps the weight of your trouble has left you feeling very lonely. Jesus knew so well what it was to feel abandoned. He also knew that you would be facing trying times and lonely hours in your own life. That is why He prayed that I might send a special Friend, Comforter, Helper, and Guide to dwell in your heart and be with you as long as you live.

I am speaking now of the Holy Spirit. This Spirit Friend I send to you is not separate from My will or My way. His voice will never contradict My Word, for He is at one with Me and with My Son. That is why, when you wait in silence to hear Him, He will whisper My words to you. So talk to Me in prayer, My precious child, and learn to listen for the answers My Holy Spirit will bring to you from Me. When you hear His silent words in your heart, you will surely know that I am with you.

Listen to my Spirit,
God

In Me
There Is Healing

I am the Lord who heals you.

EXODUS 15:26

He was hated and rejected by people.
He had much pain and suffering.
People would not even look at him.
He was hated, and we didn't even notice him.

ISAIAH 53:3

Child of Mine,

I know how difficult it is to move forward when you are caught in a sad spiral of memories and regrets. Some days you find yourself wondering, How long can this last? Will it never end? Know this: The only way through this heartache is right up the middle. There is no bypass, no shortcut. You cannot legislate its boundaries or force it over the finish line.

So don't keep trying to give your heart ultimatums. Trust Me when I tell you that you are right where you need to be today. What you are experiencing has touched many, many lives before you and will touch many, many more, for grief is a part of the human journey. Your parents and grandparents and great-grandparents knew grief, as did every generation. To live a fully human life is to experience grief. Even My own sinless Son was not exempt from it. He was a man of sorrows, well acquainted with grief.

So walk on steadily. But believe this: In Me there is healing and wholeness and hope for tomorrow.

Trust Me and see,
God

I Have Sought You Out and Found You

He found them in a desert, a windy, empty land.
He surrounded them . . . guarding them . . . like an
eagle building its nest that flutters over its young.

DEUTERONOMY 32:10-11

Have mercy on me, O God, have mercy on
me. . . . I will take refuge in the shadow of
your wings until the disaster has passed.

PSALM 57:1 NIV

God, your love is so precious! You protect
people in the shadow of your wings.

PSALM 36:7

Dear Child,

I know where your heart is dwelling now—in a barren desert land. See, I have sought you out. I have come into this solitary place of pain and found you. Now, if only you will let Me, I will hide you in My mercy and provide for you from My endless storehouse of compassion.

While your heart is hurting, I will guard you as My own. Like an eagle protects its young, I will spread My mighty wings of protection over you and shield you from the raging winds of your affliction. While you are weak, I will carry you. I will fill your emptiness with courage and wisdom so you will be refueled and restored. Do not fear this desert time, for I am here, My child.

Your Protector,
God

I Am Your Rock and Redeemer

I myself am the Lord; I am the only Savior.

ISAIAH 43:11

The Lord, the king of Israel, is the Lord
All-Powerful. . . . This is what he says: "I am the
beginning and the end. I am the only God.
Don't be afraid! Don't worry! I have
always told you what will happen.
You are my witnesses. There is no
other God but me. I know of no
other Rock; I am the only One."

ISAIAH 44:6, 8

Dear Child,

You see the storm clouds gathering above you now, and the waves of circumstance are crashing all around. You find yourself wondering where your life went wrong. Perhaps you thought that following Me would ensure blue skies and sunny weather.

Hear My voice speaking to your heart, My child. Every life will have its storms. Remember that, and do not be surprised when they arise. The promise is not an absence of storms. The promise is that in the midst of life's inevitable hurricanes, I will be your Savior. I will be the Rock on which you stand when all else is swept away; for I am the first and the last, and there is no God besides Me. Do not fear or be afraid. The rock of My love will withstand the winds of your storm!

Steadfastly,
God

I Speak in a Quiet, Gentle Voice

Tear open the skies and come down
to earth so that the mountains shall
tremble before you. . . . Then
all nations will shake with fear
when they see you.

ISAIAH 64:1-2

Acceptance

My Dear Child,

Do you sometimes feel that My back is turned to you? Do you long for Me to tear the skies open and show you My face? Oh, My child, I have not turned away from you. I am right here.

But I am not speaking to you today in violent winds or earthquakes or fires. I am whispering to you in a quiet, gentle voice. It is a voice that can be heard not with your ears but with your heart. You will hear it best when you are very still and listen. Pull away from the great clamor of competing noises in your world. Tune out the jumbled sound of conflicting voices. Turn off the television set. Turn off the radio. Go alone to a quiet place and know that I will meet you there. It can be on a beach or in a meadow, on a mountaintop or by a stream. Or it can be in your own bedroom with the door closed.

You see, I am always talking to you, telling you of My love, giving you My guidance. But you are not always listening. So today find that place. Settle down and tell Me your feelings. Share your deepest needs. Then be very still and listen with your heart.

I want to talk to you,
God

Dare to Hope

"I know what I am planning for you,"
says the Lord. "I have good plans for you,
not plans to hurt you. I will give you
hope and a good future."

JEREMIAH 29:11

God has made us what we are.
In Christ Jesus, God made us to do
good works, which God planned in
advance for us to live our lives doing.

EPHESIANS 2:10

Dear Child,

In your present circumstances, you may sometimes feel close to despair. To despair is to send forth your imagination and choose to believe the potential negative in your circumstances. But I am asking you not to despair, but to hope instead. To hope is to send forth your imagination and choose to believe the potential positive in your circumstances.

To despair is to say you are alone and no one cares and there will never be any joy in your life again. To hope is to acknowledge that I care deeply and have a plan for your life, that I am beside you and will never leave you, that though things will never be exactly the same, there are many good times ahead for you.

What is My plan for you? My plan will unfold gradually in My perfect season. But trust this for now: It is a plan for good and not for evil. It is a plan embroidered with the beauty of My mercy in all the colors of My love. Can you hope in this? Can you choose to believe that these things will come to pass because I have told you so?

Dare to hope, My child,
God

I Am Your Shield

Many are saying about me,
"God won't rescue him."
But, Lord, you are my shield,
my wonderful God who gives me courage.
I will pray to the Lord,
and he will answer me from his
holy mountain.
I can lie down and go to sleep,
and I will wake up again,
because the Lord gives
me strength.

PSALM 3:2-5

Dearest Child,

Some of your friends who do not know Me as you do may think you are putting too much confidence in Me. They may feel that you should "come back down to the ground" and deal with reality. What they do not understand is that I am the only reality. And only when your feet are planted in My truth are you standing on solid ground.

So let them say what they will. But you know, and will continue to know, that I am your Shield and the Source of your courage. I hear every small whisper of your heart, and I answer you. I hold you in safety while you sleep, and I am right by your side when you wake up, giving you strength for the day. So keep believing in Me.

I am your Shield,
God

I Love You Forever

Can anything separate us from the love
Christ has for us? Can troubles or problems
or sufferings or hunger or nakedness or
danger or violent death?

But in all these things we have full victory through
God who showed his love for us. Yes, I am sure that
neither death, nor life, nor angels, nor ruling spirits,
nothing now, nothing in the future, no powers, nothing
above us, nothing below us, nor anything
else in the whole world will ever
be able to separate us from the love of
God that is in Christ Jesus our Lord.

ROMANS 8:35, 37-39

My Dear Child,

There is something blazing in My heart that I yearn for you to know and hold on to. And this is it: My love, which came down to you in the person of My perfect Son, Jesus, is complete, full, unchangeable, and eternal. It is the one gift that circumstances can neither alter nor steal away.

Nothing you will face in this life is powerful enough to come between you and My love for you. There is no tragedy, no sorrow, no hardship or adversity that can pull it under or wear it out. Nothing natural or supernatural, nothing dead or alive, nothing in the present or the future can ever erode it or corrupt it or cause it to budge a single inch!

My love will be your one constant in the shifting landscape of a transient universe. It is an open door when you are hungry and homeless, a warm embrace when you are lost and alone. It is a safe harbor when you are tossed by the storms of life and a roaring fire when the world has turned you out in the cold. So hold this truth as a treasure in your heart.

I love you forever!
God

Mourn with the Promise of Tomorrow

I will change their sadness into happiness; I will give them comfort and joy instead of sadness.

JEREMIAH 31:13

Acceptance

My Own Dear Child,

Today you may feel that all hope of happiness has been extracted from your heart. Because of your sadness, the future looms ahead of you like a dark and unknown corridor in which every door is closed. But believe Me today when I tell you that I am able to lead you from this shadow of mourning into a bright season of gladness. I am able to guide you through the heaviness of your sorrow into a place of deep joy.

Put your hand in Mine, as a small child puts her tiny hand into the great, rough hand of her strong, adoring dad; for I am truly a Father to you. I will lead you into that corridor called "someday." And together you and I will light the lamps and fling wide the doors of your future. So mourn now while it is time for mourning. But mourn with the promise of tomorrow.

Your Strong, Adoring Father,
God

Healed to Be a Healer

Praise be to the God and Father of our
Lord Jesus Christ. God is the Father who
is full of mercy and all comfort. He comforts
us every time we have trouble, so when
others have trouble, we can comfort them
with the same comfort God gives us.

2 CORINTHIANS 1:3-4

Dear Child of Mine,

I am the God of all comfort. I will hold you in arms of compassion and sing you My healing song of grace. I will touch the wounds within you, and in My perfect season, I will lift you from this place of pain.

But I want you to know that as I am healing you, I am also creating within you a healing ministry of your own. For to be healed by Me is to be made a healer. You see, the very comfort that I am working into your broken heart through the power of My words and the love of My people is meant to be recycled. Someday when your heart has grown strong again, I will send someone into your life who is as broken as you are today. And the compassion I am pouring into you now will flow from you to that hurting soul.

You will know how to comfort him because you will have been where he is. You will resonate with his pain. You will reach into the depth of your own healing and love him back to life for Me. What a precious vessel you will be to Me then—a vessel once humbled and hurt, and then healed to be a healer!

This is My plan for you,
God

Come, Enter My Rest

God has left us the promise that
we may enter his rest.

HEBREWS 4:1

Come near to God and he will come near to you.

JAMES 4:8 NIV

"Come to me, all of you who are tired and
have heavy loads, and I will give you rest.
Accept my teachings and learn from me, because
I am gentle and humble in spirit, and you will find
rest for your lives. The teaching that I ask you to
accept is easy; the load I give you to carry is light."

MATTHEW 11:28-30

Dearest Child,

Hear Me in your heart as I call to you, "Come now, and enter my rest." Do not constantly rush around in a mindless kind of busyness, thinking you can mask your pain. The wounds you bear must be cleansed and dressed and given time to mend.

Come daily to Me, for in My presence healing happens. Write on your calendar a special time for us to meet each day, and I will be there. Prepare a special place—a restful place where in the stillness you can hear My heart. Make it beautiful and welcoming; light a candle or bring a vase of flowers. Bring My Word to read, for it contains messages of hope and healing.

Then come expectantly, saying, "It is time to meet the One who knows me best and loves me most!" In this restful place of beauty, I will meet you every day and make you whole.

Come, rest in Me,
God

Hold Tight to This Promise

Now you are sad, but I will see you
again and you will be happy, and
no one will take away your joy.

JOHN 16:22

Nothing that God judges guilty will be
in that city. The throne of God and of
the Lamb will be there, and God's
servants will worship him.

REVELATION 22:3

Dear Child,

The fickle world you live in gives happiness with one hand and snatches it back with the other. One moment you are on top of the world, and the next the rug is pulled out from under you. Desperate people are searching everywhere for some sort of security, but there is none to be found in this temporary world.

Instead you have accepted a truth that many of these desperate ones have rejected. You have accepted the truth that the only lasting security to be found is in Me. The only ironclad promises are found in My Word. So as you are struggling with the pain this life has dealt you, remember that there is a world beyond this one.

Remember, too, these words of My Son: "Now you are sad, but I will see you again and you will be happy, and no one will take away your joy." Though He spoke these words many years ago to His disciples, they were also meant for you today. They speak hope into your present situation. For not only is Jesus with you in the struggles of today, but He is also waiting for you in a time and place where there will be total, irrevocable joy forever.

Hold tight to this promise!
God

I See Beyond Your Heartache

The One who was sitting on the
throne said, "Look! I am making
everything new!" Then he said,
"Write this, because these
words are true and can be trusted."

REVELATION 21:5

Acceptance

My Precious Child,

*To see your circumstances with temporal, human
eyes is to see heartache, tragedy, reason for regret. I
know that, for I see it too. But with My eternal eyes I
can see more. I can see beyond your heartache to your
healing, beyond your regret to your renewal, beyond
your tragedy to your triumph. For, you see, I am
constantly at work in the child who has trusted all to
Me—at work healing, changing, renewing.*

*I long for all of My children to know that I am
committed to taking the bad, the tragic, the evil things
that come into their lives and using them to bring
about good things. I am committed to redeeming every
failure or injury or wrong. And what is more, I am
using each human heartache to remold you more and
more into the image of My Son. Please, My child, keep
these truths tucked away in your heart. And in the
midst of this trying time, remember: Not one tear will
be wasted.*

Trust Me and see,
God

Come into the Sunlight

For you who honor me, goodness will shine
on you like the sun, with healing in its rays.

MALACHI 4:2

The sun will no longer be your light during the
day nor will the brightness from the moon be
your light, because the Lord will be your light
forever, and your God will be your glory. Your
sun will never set again, and your moon will
never be dark because the Lord will be your
light forever, and your time of sadness will end.

ISAIAH 60:19-20

Dearest Child,

My love for you is as powerful as the sun that rises on a misty morning. Just as the rays of the sun can burn away the fog that hangs in the morning air, the bright, warm rays of My love can burn through the clouds of despair and depression that hover about your heart.

Don't be afraid. Don't give up. I am here—very near to you in your sorrow. I am present in your pain. So instead of pulling away and isolating your wounded spirit from My love, open your heart to Me. Unlike the sun's rays, there is no way you can get too much of My healing love. The longer you soak in My Word and bathe in My Spirit, the stronger you will become. So come often into My presence, child of Mine, and open your heart to the healing rays of My love.

Bask in My love,
God

I Have Sent You a Message

Everything that was written in the past was
written to teach us. The Scriptures give us patience
and encouragement so that we can have hope.
Patience and encouragement come from God.

ROMANS 15:4-5

I have taken your words to heart so
I would not sin against you.
Your word is like a lamp for my feet
and a light for my path.

PSALM 119:11, 105

Dearest Child,

There is so much I want you to know, so many secrets I long to tell you. That is why I have sent you a message. It was sent through the hands and hearts and lives of long-ago pilgrims who knew, as you know, what it is to be broken and bruised and in need of a friend on the journey of life. These pilgrims have danced for joy in the fellowship of My Spirit and have cried out in need and found Me there.

This message, bound in a Book, tells the story of My love affair with My people. It can be a road map for your feet and a fire for your spirit when your faith grows dim. It can bring patience and perseverance when you are close to quitting. It can bring encouragement that fans the flames of hope and comfort and heals the wounded heart. Oh, My child, come. Read My Word and know Me better.

Your Loving Father,
God

Will You Choose Life?

Today I ask heaven and earth to be witnesses.
I am offering you life or death, blessings or curses.
Now, choose life! . . . To choose life
is to love the Lord your God, obey him,
and stay close to him. He is your life.

DEUTERONOMY 30:19-20

My Child,

Your struggle has been long. Your heartache has been heavy. You have cried and questioned and laid your heart on the altar of sorrows. I have been here with you through it all, as I will always be with you.

But I am asking you today to make this choice: the choice to go on. For it is a choice in the end that only you can make—a choice to walk in the land of the living, to feel the sunshine and smile at the children, to be alive! A choice to believe that in spite of your loss and all it has cost you, there is much beauty and joy just outside your heart, and it's waiting to be invited in. I have good plans for you, My child, if only you will choose to embrace them. They are plans rich with a new hope and a good future.

There are people I love out there in that place called "the future" who need what only you can give them—your smile, your wisdom, your comfort, your personality. Will you trust Me to lead you to that good place? We will travel there together, one step at a time. I will be right beside you. Will you choose life?

Your Loving Father,
God

Trust My Spirit's Power

The Spirit helps us with our weakness. We do not know how to pray as we should. But the Spirit himself speaks to God for us, even begs God for us with deep feelings that words cannot explain. God can see what is in people's hearts. And he knows what is in the mind of the Spirit, because the Spirit speaks to God for his people in the way God wants.

ROMANS 8:26-27

Acceptance

Dearest Child,

Sometimes when your heart is like a desert, words dry up. There seems to be no way to express or explain the huge, aching vacuum inside. But, please, don't let an inability to express your feelings keep you from prayer. Even if you can't find the words, come to Me. Sit with Me. Let me hold you. And we will ask My Holy Spirit to express those words that are hidden in your broken heart.

It is My Spirit's job to help you when you're weak and inarticulate. He is a Friend who will stand between us and help us hear each other. So never stay away because you lack the words. Come, trusting His power to speak for you. And also come believing that He will help you hear My voice.

I wait for you,
God

Look to the Light

Lord, I have called out to you for help; every
morning I pray to you. Lord, why do you reject me?
Why do you hide from me? You have taken away
my loved ones and friends. Darkness is my only friend.

PSALM 88:13-14, 18

They will not need the light of a lamp
or the light of the sun, because the
Lord God will give them light.

REVELATION 22:5

My Child,

Have your eyes at times been so filled with tears that you could not see Me in the midst of your circumstances? You must believe that I am always here. My love encircles and upholds you. You are My precious one. And although you may feel consumed with sadness, although you may even feel at times that the darkness is your only friend, I am asking you to believe in the Light.

Yes, there is Light at the end of this tunnel. And on the day when I take your hand and lead you out, you will again rejoice in the clear, sweet light of My joy. But until you reach that place, I will be here, shining in the midst of your darkest days, closer to you than any friend or brother. So, open your eyes of faith, My child, and . . .

Look to the Light,
God

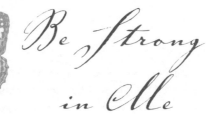

Be Strong
in Me

Finally, be strong in the Lord
and in his mighty power.

EPHESIANS 6:10 NIV

The Lord is faithful and will give
you strength and will protect you
from the Evil One.

2 THESSALONIANS 3:3

Dear Child of Mine,

I want you to be strong in Me. Yes, I know you do not feel strong now. That is why I am not asking you to be strong in your own strength. Rather I am asking you to be strong in Me.

Your own strength is as different from Mine as night is from day. Your own strength is limited and frail. My strength is limitless and infinitely powerful. Your own strength can be diminished when faced with painful circumstances. My strength in you is not reduced in the slightest by your circumstances. In fact, when you are at your weakest, that is when My strength in you is at its strongest.

So even though you feel very weak and vulnerable now, remember who dwells within you. Remember whose strength is at the very core of your being. And in the midst of your weakest hour, you will be strong in Me!

Your Source of Power,
God

I Am the Lord of All Seasons

Look, the winter is past; the rains are over
and gone. Blossoms appear through all the land.
The time has come to sing; the cooing of doves
is heard in our land. There are young figs
on the fig trees, and the blossoms on the
vines smell sweet. Get up, my darling;
let's go away, my beautiful one.

SONG OF SOLOMON 2:11-13

120

Dear Child of Mine,

Have you felt as if you were caught in the clutches of winter, held in the icy hand of hopelessness? As you survey your future, does it seem to stretch out before you like the drab, colorless contours of a frozen field? Oh, My child, trust in Me.

Just as there are seasons in creation, so are there seasons of the soul. In time, as you rest in Me and allow Me to heal you, you will feel the frozen ground in your life beginning to thaw. You will feel the days warming and the sorrow melting away as the colors of new life begin to break through. You will smell the fragrance of flowers and feel the warm wind blowing through the windows of your soul.

And then you will hear Me speaking to your spirit in a still small voice, saying, "Come, My child, My precious one. Wake up! Spring has come at last, and it is time now for you to move on. Take my hand, and together let us move out into the beauty of this new day." For, you see, I will be there for you in the warm, spring breezes just as I have been with you in the icy winter winds.

I am the Lord of all seasons,
God

See Your Healing Spring Forth

Share your food with the hungry and bring poor,
homeless people into your own homes. When you
see someone who has no clothes, give him yours,
and don't refuse to help your own relatives. . .
Then your light will shine like the dawn,
and your wounds will quickly heal. . . .
The Lord will always lead you.
He will satisfy your needs in dry lands
and give strength to your bones.
You will be like a garden that has much water,
like a spring that never runs dry.

ISAIAH 58:7-8, 11

My Child,

The most healing thing in the world is loving others. Indeed, the most healing thing you can do for yourself at times is to set aside your own need temporarily and reach out to meet the needs of someone else. Just put your grief in a drawer for a morning—it will wait for you! Or let Me hold it for you for a few hours so you can go out, unencumbered, into the world of human need.

Look at someone else's pain, someone else's grief, someone else's need, and simply do what you can to bring healing and comfort. Do something practical to meet that need. And when you return to your own pain, you will find that some small part of it has been lifted as you focused on someone else.

Choosing to love, even when you feel you have very little to give, is a way of connecting with My boundless source of love. It is a way of tapping into My spring of healing water that never runs dry. In some mysterious sense, it is a way of being the healer and the one being healed at the same time. So risk loving, My child, and . . .

See your healing spring forth,
God

I Will Be for You
a Quiet Consolation

Those who are sad now are happy,
because God will comfort them.

MATTHEW 5:4

I will make an agreement with them that will last
forever. I will never turn away from them; I will
always do good to them. I will make them want to
respect me so they will never turn away from me.

JEREMIAH 32:40

Dear Child,

In your mournful season, I have been for you a quiet consolation. In the valley of the shadow, I have been for you the narrow road to higher ground. In your time of lamenting, I have been for you the shoulder of a friend.

When you looked, you found Me there, nearer to you than ever you dared to dream. When you listened, you heard the quiet music of My Spirit deep within you—a song of blessing, a song of release. You reached out your hand as a blind man, not knowing who was there, and as you touched the hem of My garment, you felt My healing flow into you. You called My name, and I answered, "Yes, child. I am still here. I have been with you through it all."

Faithfully Yours,
God